my Bible ABC

A

Abraham depends on God for **A**ll things.

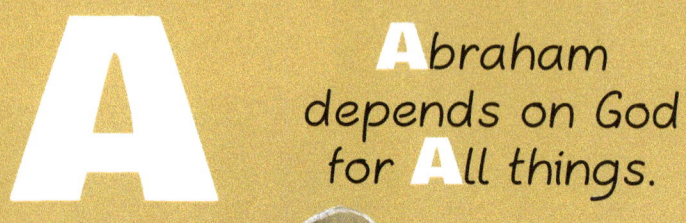

B Baby Moses is safe in a floating **B**asket.

C

God gives Moses the commandments on 2 stone tablets.

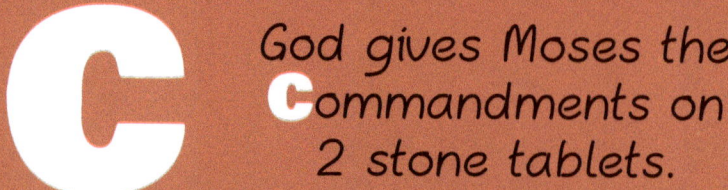

D

Daniel prays and is saved in a **D**en of lions.

E

The birds feed **E**lijah **E**verything he needs.

F

Uh oh! Adam and Eve eat the Forbidden Fruit.

G

Gideon obeys
God's plan. Toot, toot,
Goes the trumpet.

Hannah is Happy
for her baby boy.

Cute baby Isaac Is born.

J

Joseph **J**ust got a colorful new coat.

King Jesus is born in a stable, where animals are **K**ept.

L

A **L**ittle boy shares his **L**unch with Jesus.

M
Mary and **M**artha learn from Jesus.

Noah **N**eeds God's help to build a giant boat.

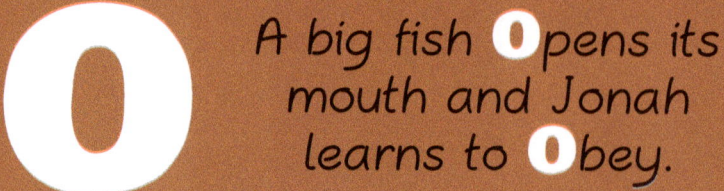

O

A big fish **o**pens its mouth and Jonah learns to **o**bey.

P

Paul shares the good news with the People.

Q

Queen Esther saves her people.

R Ruth Runs to stay with Naomi.

S

Samuel listens to God's **S**oft voice.

T

Jesus Teaches at the Temple.

U
Jesus goes Up, up, Up to Heaven.

V

With God's help, little David shouts "Victory!"

W

Wisemen
Willingly bring gifts to Jesus.

X

The Holy Spirit gives e**x**tra power.

Y

Jesus loves
You very much.

Z zacchaeus is sorry.

More books from iCharacter.org

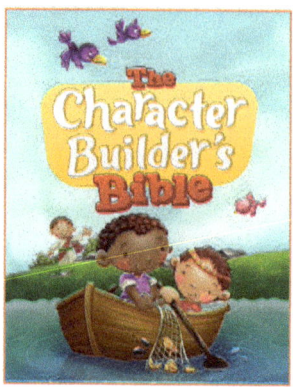

Published by iCharacter Ltd. (Ireland)
www.iCharacter.org
By Agnes de Bezenac
Illustrated by Agnes de Bezenac
Colored by Noviyanti W., Hanny A., Gabriela C. and Henny Y.
Copyright 2019. All rights reserved.
Copyright © 2019 by iCharacter Ltd. All rights reserved. No part of this book may be reproduced in any form or by any electronic or mechanical means, including information storage and retrieval systems, without written permission from the publisher or author, except in the case of a reviewer, who may quote brief passages embodied in critical articles or in a review.

www.ingramcontent.com/pod-product-compliance
Lightning Source LLC
Chambersburg PA
CBHW061811070526
44586CB00024B/2804